Peter Case, PhD

(former Summerhill pupil)

CHILDROME

SUMMERHILL AND BEYOND

How to give freedom from compulsory school and self-government to every child in national education

IMPRINT

Author:
Peter Case, PhD
Address:
Dorfblick 7E
CH-3538 Röthenbach
Switzerland
Tel.
+41(0)79 126 48 44
Email:
peter.case@mhsmail.ch
Web:
www.childrome.com

───────────────────────────

CONTENTS

ACKNOWLEDGEMENTS

PREFACE 9

INTRODUCTION 20

CHAPTER 1: Application of Summerhill Principles to the National Education System .. 53

CHAPTER 2:   The New Free Schools 61

CHAPTER 3: Child Dignity in Education 83

CHAPTER 4: Purpose of Education 89

CHAPTER 5: Historical Concepts of Education 98

CHAPTER_6: Compulsory School 105

CHAPTER 7: The Need for a New Element in the Education System 123

CHAPTER 8: The German Hort 140

CHAPTER 9: Empowerment 145

CHAPTER 10: Structure of the Childromes .. 147

CHAPTER 11: Countries where Childromes may be Needed 165

CHAPTER 12: Introduction of Childromes into the Existing School System 170

POSTSCRIPT 178

ABOUT THE AUTHOR 189
LITERATURE 192
FURTHER READING 203

ACKNOWLEDGEMENTS

First, I wish to express my acknowledgement to the following persons and institutions:

my parents for sending me to Summerhill and somehow finding the money to do so;

my sister, Sue, for her insightful and precise comments on several parts of the text; my late brother, Don, for numerous in-depth discussions on a wide range of topics from education to politics, my daughter, Isabel, for her insistence - even as a child - on my writing this book. as well as other members of our family and friends for their ideas and comments. All I can hope is that I have been able to live up to their expectations.

Fritjof Capra for his advanced thought on a new paradigm for science and society, and the late Steve Jobs for developing the iPhone, on which parts of this book were written, and finally the university library in Freiburg i. Br. (Germany) for allowing me to pursue my studies there.

My special thanks are due to Sam Jordison of Writers' Workshop for his professional assessment of the manuscript, which has helped me to greatly improve its presentation and structure.

PREFACE

Historically, our education system has evolved under the iron dictate of compulsory school, which has been retained in deference to the fallacious belief that children will only learn if forced to do so. Today, the need for the state to provide some form of education infrastructure is undisputed: controversial is only the very much more difficult question of what its objectives should be and how it should be designed. In my view, there is a desperate need to restrain schools from terrorising children with their detestable examination rituals and assessment routines.

In his book Deschooling Society, Ivan Illich was so exasperated with conventional schools that he proposed eradicating them. The approach I propose is more constructive in that it gives schools a new role and doesn't simply intend to get rid of them.

The outspoken Swedish educational reformer Ellen Key (1849-1926) was especially concerned about the negative effects of conventional schools, and sought a way to alleviate them. She was very critical of the situation in Swedish schools at the end of the 19th century. Ellen Key saw the child as a sapling, complete in itself, that only needed to grow in stature. For healthy development, it only needed a suitable substrate and the right conditions. She was adamant that the child naturally creates its own system of values and does not need the straight jacket of school discipline and obligatory learning.

I would like to see a change of heart in public education along the lines she proposed, according to which the child would better be left alone to develop in its own way. One day I had a flash of inspiration: maybe the time is ripe for something really new and exciting, that could transform the whole concept of school and education! Something that has never been tried before, that has the potential to redeem us from the endless round of failure and disenchantment; at long last put human life right at the centre of interest. Indeed, why not something along the lines of A.S. Neill's renowned Summerhill school, where lessons are voluntary and the pupils have their own parliament. In other words: *actually, to apply* the principles of Summerhill school to the whole national education system!

Alongside the schools, the book proposes the introduction of a new facility, a so-called "children's drome", or "chil-drome", to assume the responsibility for today's sadly neglected *emotional and social* aspects of education, and provides step-by-step guidance on the political, legal and practical measures needed.

The book includes a critical appraisal of

the existing school situation in England in the wake of a succession of government reforms intended to raise learning standards, and proposes close cooperation between the childromes and schools in providing a *full programme of education* in place of the inadequate arrangements currently in place.

As a former pupil in Summerhill, I feel well-qualified to propose a reform along these lines.

INTRODUCTION

Summerhill was the brainchild of Alexander Sutherland Neill, a Scottish school teacher who sought an alternative to the repressive school system of his time, particularly in Scotland. Neill wrote several books covering his experiences as a teacher – for a review see footnote[1] or Lit. (1). Inspired by the work of Homer Lane (2), who had experimented with child self-government, Neill finally opened a school of his own, later named "Summerhill". – Summerhill, a boarding

[1] http://www.summerhill-school.co.uk/books-by-asneill.php (accessed 01.05.2015)

school, was based on the conviction that children would best develop into responsible, creative and happy individuals if they were given the chance to grow up free from "moulding" by parents and teachers. To this end, Neill instituted a children's parliament to regulate school affairs, in which all pupils had an equal say. Most important of all: lessons were made available on a purely voluntary basis.

My parents had sent me to Summerhill after becoming dissatisfied with local schools. On arriving home from school one afternoon, and seeing my mother, I burst into tears because the teacher had rapped my knuckles with his ruler for laying my hands on his desk during class, which, unknown to me, was contrary to school rules. At first I hadn't realised at all what I was supposed to have done wrong!

As a child, Summerhill always seemed right to me, and I was fully in accord with its principles as I understood them. Voluntary lessons seemed to me obviously right, and that pupils and teachers were on a level and had the same rights seemed only natural. It filled me with horror and dismay that other schoolchildren of my age were forced to attend school and were called by their surnames. For those readers interested in having a first-hand account what it was really like at Summerhill, I warmly suggest consulting the reports by my former school colleague, the journalist Angela Neustatter, in The

Guardian newspaper[2]:

and by former Summerhill pupil and author Mikey Cuddihy in her delightful, extremely well-written and highly readable book (3):

From cover text:

[2]http://www.theguardian.com/uk/1999/may/30/theobserver.uknews7 (accessed 04. 2015)

When Mikey Cuddihy was orphaned at the age of 9, her life exploded. She and her siblings were sent from New York to board at experimental Summerhill School, in Suffolk, and abandoned there.

A child left alone and far from home, Mikey navigated this strange world of permissiveness and neglect, forging an identity almost in defiance of it. A Conversation About Happiness is a vivid and intense memoir of coming of age amidst the unravelling social experiment of sixties and seventies Britain.

Mikey Cuddihy recounts:

"'Who's that funny old man with the

dog?' I ask a freckle-faced girl who looks like she knows her way around.

I keep seeing a tall man in a brown corduroy jacket and baggy old man's jeans, the kind that carpenters wear. On his feet are enormous shiny black lace-ups. He's stooped and has a strange accent. I think he must be German.

He's surrounded by a group of small children who are jumping up at him, shouting, 'Neill! Neill!'

He looks down, keeping a lighted cigarette out of their way.

You, you and you, go and find me a great big man with white hair who's been seen wandering around the school. He's an awfully nice-looking chap!'

'It's you! It's you! You're the man with the white hair!' they all shout, laughing excitedly.

Evie turns to me and smiles: 'Oh, that's Neill. This is his school.'

'What, you mean he's the principal?'

'I guess, well, the headmaster, but not like a normal head. I mean, he doesn't order us around or tell us what to do.'

'Sometimes he says things at the meeting, but he has to put his hand up and wait for the chairman to call his name before he can speak, like everyone else.'

The Guardian review of Mikey's book by Christopher Turner can be found at footnote[3].

[3] http://www.theguardian.com/books/2014/mar/28/conversation-happiness-summerhill-school-review-mikey-cuddihy#img-1 (accessed 04. 2015)

I often thought: is there no way of applying Summerhill ideas to the national school system to give all children a more exhilarating school experience, so that they derive far more benefit from it than at present? In fact, the present book is a late result of these my thoughts and feelings as a child.

On several occasions, both before and after I left Summerhill, Neill requested me (contrary to the normal rotational practice) to chair the weekly meeting of staff and children. Moreover, Neill had numerous prolonged meetings with my father, Howard W. Case (4), an English teacher and specialist in behavioural disorders ("maladjustment"), at which fundamental educational issues were discussed. My father and I often discussed the meaning of freedom in education, my father pointing out that "freedom" in the sense of "freedom from" was a negative term and by no means self-explanatory, and therefore required closer definition (for example by describing the objectives and content of the proposed educational scheme). From this resulted the suggestion to Neill to write a new book on the theory and practice of freedom in child education, a book he did in fact consider writing. However, instead of that he decided to have one of his existing books relaunched abroad. In 1969 the German publisher Rowohlt brought out " Theorie und Praxis der antiautoritären Erziehung" (Theory and Practice of Anti-Authoritarian Education) (5) – a translation of the English: "Summerhill A Radical Approach to Child Rearing" (6). Like his other books, this was again a rambling narrative of Neill's educational experiences, and did not at all live up to the term "theory". Notwithstanding, the book was jubilantly received by the German press and public and triggered off a wide and enduring discussion on Neill's purported concept of education, whereby unfortunately, the debate circled mainly around the term "anti-authoritarian" introduced by the publisher (a term Neill had never used himself), and finally exhausted itself in generalities.

These experiences strengthened my resolve to do all I could to further and uphold Neill's educational legacy, if possible by finding a way to apply Summerhill principles to the national school system. This endeavour continued to occupy me during my research work on fluid dynamics at Liverpool University. As soon as the research work was finished I began writing down the educational ideas which had come to me by then. In keeping with my work at the university, I was concerned to put these on a scientific basis, and I continued work on the concept with a programme of research at the university library in Freiburg i. Br. (Germany) around 1980.

The task confronting me to reform the national education system was to use Summerhill principles in a way that would preserve the main features of Summerhill without incurring the penalty of parental separation inevitably associated with a boarding school setup.

Initially, I had envisaged a complex restructuring of national education. In the end, a fairly uncomplicated solution presented itself, involving the introduction – alongside the school and the parental home – of a "third instance", which I have termed a "children's drome" - or "childrome", to emphasise its commitment to the furthering of children of school age (for details see chapter 1).

At present, efforts are underway by the British government to restructure the national school system out of a concern to raise learning standards by the introduction of a new class of schools, the new free schools (for a description, see chapter 2).

The total picture with the childromes and schools would be quite similar to what we have at Summerhill, with one decisive difference, that under the new system, pupils could continue to live with their parents. I do not believe Neill took this need seriously enough. In other words, whilst Neill gave children the freedom to live their own lives, at the same time he took away their freedom to grow up with their parents. Summerhill in its present form has outlived its purpose. As a boarding school, it still does not reply adequately to the expectations and educational needs of the present. Recent changes (see footnote[4]) are a step in the right direction that could solve the problem of parental

---
[4] Admission of day pupils

separation for children whose parents live near the school. Today, Summerhill is run by Neill's daughter and former Summerhill pupil, Zoë Neill Readhead.

In what follows, Chapter 1 poses the question of how to apply Summerhill principles to the national school system. Chapters 2-6 discuss fundamental aspects of today's national school system and the need for change.

The need for a new element in the education system is discussed in Chapter 7. The German *hort*, an early forerunner of childrome, is described in Chapter 8.

The remaining chapters provide details of

the proposed childromes, their setting up, and working.

P. Case

Röthenbach im Emmental, Switzerland

2016

CHAPTER 1: APPLICATION OF SUMMERHILL PRINCIPLES TO THE NATIONAL EDUCATION SYSTEM

As mentioned earlier, the concept to apply Summerhill ideas to the national education system is simple in principle. However, the following snags had to be overcome.

For one, boarding schools such as Summerhill carry the penalty that children are separated for long periods from their parents, so this feature had to be excluded. For this reason, too, the idea to set up Summerhill *replicas* across the entire country had to be rejected. Further, traditional schools cannot simply be converted to the Summerhill system – for example by introducing freedom from lessons – since this would involve a far too crass break with custom.

To overcome these problems, I adopted a two-pronged approach, i.e. by first dividing Summerhill's functions into two main areas: a social area; and a school (i.e. learning) area. These two functions I then apportioned to two other institutions, a new "children's drome", yet to be set up, and the existing schools. The "children's drome" - or "childrome", would assume responsibility for the emotional and social aspects of education (see chapter 4).

A few years before he died, Neill told me he thought it worthwhile to follow up the childrome concept, of which he had learnt from a rough first draft of mine.

In this concept, the content and quantity

of learning considered to be in the child's best interests would be decided jointly by child, parents, childrome and school – with the possible proviso that the child attend agreed school subjects for at least a complete school term. The possibility must also be borne in mind that the child, understandably, might decide not to attend school at all!

No lessons would be held in the childrome itself, and during school hours, children would return to the childrome after completing their lessons. The total picture with the childromes and schools would be quite similar to what we have at Summerhill, with one decisive difference, that under the new system, pupils could continue to live with their parents.

CHAPTER 2:
THE NEW FREE SCHOOLS

Before going into details of the new free schools, permit me to outline the English school system as it existed prior to the recent government reform.

The English school system is based on the concept that all children must attend school or an equivalent system from the ages of 5 to 18. The legal foundation for this is provided by the Education Act (10) and the National Curriculum. Schools are graded for different student age ranges into primary and secondary schools (alternative names used for these are infant, junior and high schools). Comprehensive schools are combined primary and secondary schools and were first introduced in the 1970s. Some comprehensive schools have as many as 6.000 students. In all schools, the educational endeavour is directed exclusively to training the intellect. The subject matter to be taught at each school stage is laid down centrally by government (e.g. in the National Curriculum) or by the local authority, but may in some cases be decided by the schools themselves. No provision is made in the Education Act for furthering social or emotional goals. Student assessment is by examination and other dedicated assessment procedures. Secondary schools issue GCSE (General Certificate of Secondary Education) qualifications, which were introduced in 1951. Higher qualifications (for example the degrees BA, BSc, MA, MSc and PhD) are issued by the universities and in some cases by the polytechnics.

The English school system, though still basically the same as it was beforehand, has been modified in part by the reform programme introduced by the government during the 20 years up to 2015. The new free schools were created in the third part of the reform.

The reform was introduced with the intention to raise learning standards in primary and secondary education, partly in response to the modest rating of English students in the European PISA[5] studies.

The **first part** of the reform involved the privatisation of primary and secondary schools under the Blair (Labour) administration (1997 to 2007).

---

[5] https://www.gov.uk/government/speeches/2012-oecd-pisa-results (accessed 04. 2015)

The **second part** involved the conversion – likewise under the Blair administration – of the older "underachieving" primary, secondary and comprehensive schools into a new class of schools known as "academies"[6] – *a very unusual name indeed for a school!*, and the creation of some new academies. The majority of academies are secondary and comprehensive

[6] http://www.politics.co.uk/reference/academies (accessed 04. 2015)

schools, but some primary schools also have academy status.[7]

The **third part** was introduced by Conservative Education Secretary Michael Gove and involved the more intensive monitoring and reporting of

[7] http://en.wikipedia.org/wiki/academy_(English_school) (accessed 04. 2015)

learning standards in the classroom. These measures were bitterly resented by teachers, who saw them as an incursion on their autonomy, and they were very doubtful of their pedagogic value, finally resulting in a teachers' revolt, in which no less than three votes of no confidence in the Education Secretary were passed by teachers' organisations, among them the influential National Union of Teachers (NUT)[8], resulting finally in Gove's replacement as Education Secretary.

[8] https://www.teachers.org.uk/edufacts/pisa (accessed 04. 2015)

Michael Gove's first unsuccessful reform programme was quickly replaced by a second, in which some of the existing academies were converted into so-called "free schools". Also, some additional free schools not based on the existing schools were set up. The free schools created under the reform and later will be referred to here as "new free schools" to differentiate them from the older free schools of Summerhill type. Like the academies, new free schools in England are non-profit-making, independent, state-funded schools which are free to attend but which are not controlled by a local authority. They have more financial and curricular freedom than the academies. The new free schools are subject to the same School Admissions Code as all other state-funded schools. The new free schools, which incidentally, have nothing to do with free schools of Summerhill type (in which the word "free" signifies freedom from lessons!), represent an interesting development in the English school landscape. For details of the new free schools, see footnote[9]. The creation of new free schools continued through 2015.

[9] http://www.bbc.com/news/education-18819391 (accessed 04. 2015)

Though acclaimed in glowing terms by their promoters, opinions are divided both on the need for, and on the effectiveness of the new free schools, as the following comments by Christine Blower, general secretary of the National Union of Teachers, show:

"There is no justification for the systematic dismantling of the English education system that we are currently witnessing.

"Free schools are neither wanted by the majority nor needed by the system, as we have seen with the Beccles free school in Suffolk. They are wreaking havoc with co-ordinated pupil placement, creating surplus places and pitching schools against each other.

"Schools are desperately short of finances yet money is being found for schools which will educate tiny numbers of children."[10]

By contrast, Rachel Wolf, director of the New Schools Network, which advises groups wanting to set up a school, says there is now "huge

---

[10] http://www.bbc.com/news/education-18819391 (accessed 04.2015)

momentum" behind the scheme. She said: "Today's announcement sees the free schools movement well on its way to delivering a great new school for every community. Many teachers and existing schools are behind the latest projects."

CHAPTER 3:
CHILD DIGNITY IN EDUCATION

A serious drawback of conventional schools is their dependence on examinations and performance assessment (marking).

These may be destructive of the dignity, self-respect and self-confidence of children, qualities that education must nurture.

The Swiss educational philosopher Johannes Giesinger finds that whilst this may be true of any educational intervention in a child's life, action acutely detrimental to a child's dignity and self-respect should if possible be avoided:

"However valuable an educational aim may be, the educator should never treat the child in a way that damages the child's capacity to see himself as having the standing to make claims."[11]. The con-

[11] http://www.erziehungsphilosophie.ch/vortraege/Giesinger-Dignity_and_Education-Vortrag.pdf (accessed 04. 2015)

cept of dignity as having the "standing to make claims" Giesinger derives indirectly from Kant: " To respect children is to treat them in a way that enables them to see themselves as persons endowed with dignity, that is as having the equal standing to make claims on others."[12] There are also disturbing reports of the use by teachers of ridicule and mockery in front of class as a means to enforce discipline.

[12] http://www.erziehungsphilosophie.ch/publikationen/Giesinger_Respect_in_Education-OA.pdf (accessed 04. 2015). My thanks are extended to Johannes Giesinger for his kind permission to quote from his publications.

For the future, therefore, the endeavour in schools should be twofold: (1) to squeeze the use of examinations and marking to an absolute minimum; (2) to dissuade teachers from employing belittling methods when enforcing discipline.

CHAPTER 4: PURPOSE OF EDUCATION

In common with Neill I am very sceptical of the official view of education as being no more than the dissemination of information. I believe for one that this is only half of the story (see below), and for another that children should in any case have a say in what they are expected to learn, i.e. that learning content should be chosen in harmony with the interests and natural aptitudes of the child and not imposed from outside.

The childrome, like Summerhill, is founded on this axiom. Furthermore, effective learning depends on motivation. Motivation itself comes from within and depends intimately on the emotional and social conditions under which the pupil is expected to learn. To reflect the much broader view of education held by Neill, I propose the following, expanded, definition of the purpose of education:

(A) Intellectual goals

Education is the process of imparting to children the intellectual tools they will need in adult life, and, to a greater or lesser extent, of aiding them to develop a critical understanding of such socio-metaphysi-

cal issues as religion, morality, humanity, health care, democracy and the arts.

(B) Emotional and Social goals

Alongside the intellectual goals of education, there are the emotional and social ones.

These encompass, among others: to strengthen children's dignity and self-respect, and aid them to cultivate the ability: (a) to achieve a contented mode of life; (b) to establish a stable, self-assured, au-

thentic personality; (c) to set and achieve desirable goals in their emotional, social and later professional lives; (d) to understand and cooperate with their fellow beings, including formation of meaningful relationships, and

(e) to contribute to, and carry responsibility for, the wellbeing of others.

For an in-depth discussion of the beginnings and historical development of educational thought, see Mayer (7). The additional function of modern education, which is to pass judgement on children and assess their worth, is a troubled issue, and it is questionable whether it can be reconciled with the proper objectives of education as outlined above.

CHAPTER 5: HISTORICAL CONCEPTS OF EDUCATION

It is apparent that from Confucius to Plato and Aristotle, right through to Rousseau and Steiner, see (8), the simple assumption was made that the child in his adult years would reflect the education provided to him, requiring that the contents of education should be chosen according to the desired qualities of the

later adult. In modern times, by the introduction of psychological concepts, Susan Isaacs and (especially) Melanie Klein, see (8), initiated a break from this assumption, whereby

Isaacs and Klein focussed not so much on child development as a whole, but primarily on learning. Significantly, the assumption of previous epochs that teaching content would automatically be reflected in adulthood was not applied to the style of education (i.e. liberal or authoritarian). Quite the reverse, there existed from earliest Greek times a tendency to apply a decidedly authoritarian style of education (7), probably in accordance with military training.

Of course, there is no proof that any particular school system would be more effective than any other. To assess this, one is in large measure dependent on intuition coupled with experience: One may ask: do these particular children become happier people/ better thinkers / more successful adults than others? There are also indications from psychotherapy that certain school situations can cause traumas that may exert a negative effect right into adulthood (9). Following Neill, I am convinced that the most promising educational systems are those that work in harmony with a child's natural development, and that Summerhill-type freedom and child self-government are the most plausible way to do this, because they (a) make room for the child to fully develop his emotional faculties; (b) provide a social environment in which to practice cooperative, democratic procedures, and (c) avoid the obstacles inherent in a repressive school system.

CHAPTER_6:
COMPULSORY SCHOOL

The 1944 Education Act (Section 36) (10) states that parents are responsible for the education of their children, "by regular attendance at school or otherwise", which allows children to be educated at home. The legislation places no requirement for parents who choose not to send their children to school to follow the National Curriculum, or to give formal lessons, or to follow school hours and terms, and parents do not need to be qualified teachers (11).

Author's Note However, these freedoms are only of a theoretical nature, since the state provides no financial support to parents who choose to educate their children outside of school.

How and when the concept of compulsory school first arose is unclear in history and has been lost in the mists of time. Details of its introduction in England and Germany are given (slightly misleadingly) in the internet under the search terms: "Origin of compulsory schooling in England", and,

"Origin of compulsory schooling in Germany." Note: the compulsion for children to attend school is founded partly in the Education Act[13] and partly in common law in England, and parents can be fined and/or prosecuted if

[13] http://www.legislation.gov.uk/ukpga/1996/56/section/7 (accessed 04. 2015)

they fail to comply with a local authority order to send their child to school[14] (i.e. if the conditions for home schooling are not given.)

In ancient Greece, intellectual and sport – or military – training were taken together.

[14] https://www.gov.uk/search?q=school+attendance. (accessed 04.2015)

In those early communities marked by incessant wars of conquest, there existed a tendency to apply a strict and authoritarian style of education. Broadly, therefore, compulsory school may have arisen in analogy with military training.

More specifically, it is known that in 335 B.C., Athens passed a law making military training compulsory for all boys on reaching the age of 18 (7), so indirectly, this could be considered as the origin of compulsory school. Note therefore that compulsory school probably developed tacitly in the wake of military training and was not part of a reasoned educational concept.

Little attention is paid to it in major works on education (8) (12). No serious doubts have been raised on the necessity for it. It has remained unchallenged in national education systems to the present day. Compulsory school has been retained not simply because of the belief that children will only learn if forced to do so, but also on quite unspectacular grounds, such as (a) to avoid parents keeping their children at home or at work, where they might lack formal education, and (b) to ensure that at all times schools are charged to capacity.

I believe freedom from lessons should

be made a cornerstone of modern education, whereas at present, compulsory lessons continue to represent a major obstacle to progress.

Owing to the pressure to complete the full curricular programme, as specified, for example, in the

National Curriculum[15], academically less interested as well as immigrant children find themselves in a vicious circle of failure, apathy and lack of self-confidence. Thus not even a minimum of competence is achieved, and the

[15] https://www.gov.uk/government/collections/national-curriculum (accessed 04. 2015)

pupil finally leaves school as a discouraged, bitter and inadequate juvenile (a serious threat to the public order). For this and other reasons, I am in favour of abolishing compulsory school – that tiresome vestige of the past!

I believe that compulsory school is the guarantor of the preferential status of intellectual education because child/parents have no alternative but to acquiesce in the academic order prescribed. I believe compulsory school should be replaced by the right to receive education in the sense intended in English law[16]. Also,

[16] http://www.loc.gov/law/help/chil

compulsory school gives the school a status so dominant and overwhelming that it sees itself legitimated to dictate educational practice and policy to society. In certain countries, a bizarre power structure has arisen on the part of

d-rights/uk.php#t49 (accessed 04. 2015)

the educational authorities, for whom democracy is a hollow word. The introduction of childromes would require power-sharing between the school and childrome authorities, leading to a détente and to normalisation of this extremely unhealthy situation.

In her book "Betrogene Kinder: Eine

Sozialgeschichte der Kindheit" (Betrayed Children: A Social History of Childhood), Erna M. Johansen paints a very depressing, truly heart-rending picture of the social situation of school children in England and Germany in the middle ages to the last century. From this it is evident that today's adults owe a much better deal to the children of the nation than they had until now.

CHAPTER 7: THE NEED FOR A NEW ELEMENT IN THE EDUCATION SYSTEM

Present-day education deprives children of the freedom to live their own lives at a time when this is important for their personal development; moreover, the neighbourhood environment, particularly in large towns, does not offer the child adequate opportunities for growth. As a result, his/her basic needs are not fully satisfied, his/her qualities are not fully developed, and important educational objectives such as vital perception, self-confidence, humanity and democratic competence are only partially achieved.

But do we know what a child's natural development would be? Questions of this nature are the precinct of developmental psychology. An interesting review of current research in this field is given in Wikipedia[17]. Furthermore, there are many

---

[17] http://en.wikipedia.org/wiki/Developmental_psy-

reports of school-related health problems suffered by school children, such as poor concentration, nervousness, bed-wetting, etc. Tragic cases of suicide have also been reported, not

chology#Social_and_emotional_development (accessed 04. 2016) only among university students, but also among school children. To ensure children can become emotionally and socially mature it makes sense to provide a structure within which they can independently pursue their interests and resolve their differences. It has been too readily assumed in the past that the state school could provide such a structure, though for financial reasons it must lack several aspects long recognised by private schools as essential (e.g. small classes). In recent times a number of educationalists – notably von Hentig (13) – have recognised that the school cannot carry the burden placed upon it for the whole of education. There are several reasons for this:

The school class is unsuited to promote social maturity because: (a) of the large size of today's schools, resulting from economic pressures; (b) the school class is conceived as a learning unit, not as a social group. For this, the age range is too narrow, class functioning is too externally dominated, and because of the sterile, anti-life atmosphere prevalent in classrooms.

Many believe that improvements are possible through changes in schools, for example through "free" classroom activity, abolition of homework, less marking, less subjects, more interchangeability between classes, more school psychologists etc. It may be that one or other of these measures with one or other teacher could make an improvement. Why they have not been introduced on a much wider scale is partly because of the pressure for academisation. It is not in the nature of schools to oppose the transmission of knowledge, or the academisation, for example, of the arts. On the contrary, the school sees its main purpose in canalising and transmitting academic knowledge, being in effect a children's university.

When the attempt is made, as for example at the Glockseeschule (14) in Hannover, to overcome some of the barriers, political forces soon lead to a clean sweep being made, and the school reverts to pursuing one objective only – namely the academic. Unfortunately, there is no institution which during school hours could provide for the remaining objectives. As Illich (15) puts it, the school has an 'educational monopoly'. It is often considered to be the task of the home to educate towards emotional and social maturity, but unfortunately, owing to the structure of the home and the fact that the abilities, needs and interests of parents and children are so different, this is frequently no better suited to the task than the school. Indeed, parents tend to deploy their superior material and verbal resources to ensure that their own needs and interests take priority.

For all these reasons prospects are poor that society could initiate a process of renewal, so the search must begin for a possible way out of the dilemma. As anyone can confirm who has ever learnt a foreign language to near-perfection, the key to successful learning is extremely strong personal motivation, coupled to the freedom to refuse or choose. The opposite – compulsion to learn – can be a deterrent.

Simply to introduce freedom from lessons would be very much against the custom in traditional schools, quite impracticable, and would probably be vehemently opposed. Since the school, as argued above, cannot carry the responsibility for the whole of education, the need arises for a second public educational facility capable of providing social and emotional education. The childrome is ideally suited to this. To avoid childrome and school becoming alienated from their conceived educational purposes, and to achieve optimum organisation, it is important that each be given full autonomy.

CHAPTER 8: THE GERMAN HORT

in Germany, so-called *hort*s (lat. *hortus*, garden) were attached to schools decades ago providing supervision and recreation. These bear a certain resemblance to childrome, but in reality their purpose is quite different.

In former Eastern Germany, the educational, social and ideological function of *horts* was emphasised. Much effort was invested in helping children to complete homework and in enforcing behavioural norms such as concentration, discipline, orderly clothing and cleanliness. In this part of the country, the *horts* were later gradually absorbed into the general school system.

In Western Germany, the principal aim of the *horts* has always been to provide a refuge after school for children whose parents are at work (Ger. *schlüsselkinder*, latchkey children). There, sociologists often expressed the desire for the *hort* to be upgraded to an educational facility supplementing the school (16) (17) (18) (19). In the main, however, the call was for larger, better staffed and equipped, *horts*. My proposal would be to go far beyond that and upgrade the *horts* to provide social and emotional education of the type envisaged for childrome.

In Germany, the *horts* were still in full operation at the time of writing.

CHAPTER 9: EMPOWERMENT

In view of the riots in 2011 in London and other cities, there is a widespread feeling that radical changes are needed in the environment of youth. To accomplish this, we should consider creating conditions in which young people's voices can be heard, giving them a say in their own affairs and enabling them to alter the conditions under which they grow up – EMPOWERMENT! It is conceivable that by this means further explosions of violence among youth could be forestalled. The introduction of childromes is a practical way to do just that.

CHAPTER 10:
STRUCTURE OF THE CHILDROMES

The legal form of the childromes could be as non-profit-making societies affiliated to a national organisation, which would establish a code of practice. On no account should childromes be regarded as a parental substitute, and parents must remain the principal educators of their children (20). In addition, in order to prevent children being exploited by uncaring parents and employers, a practice prevalent in the Middle Ages (21), education in the full sense must remain compulsory. In other words, the present legal duty to attend school needs to be transformed into the legal duty to attend the dual childrome-school system – indeed a radical innovation in education. For this, not only legislative but also administrative changes are required.

Like Summerhill, the childromes (one or several per school) would be organised on democratic lines.

They would be set up in the immediate vicinity of homes for perhaps about 100 children, who could then reach them easily on foot. All children within a prescribed geographical area should be admitted. Thus in distinction to many previous experiments, which mainly benefited the middle class, the childromes would offer local, less privileged children the opportunity to participate. To achieve an adequate staff-pupil ratio, it would be essential for a good number of parents to assist the childrome staff in their work. The increasing prevalence of parental action groups in Europe, the USA and Japan strongly suggests that many parents would be prepared and able to provide support in this way. As mentioned above, a precondition for parental participation is that the childromes be administered jointly by parents and staff. These could where necessary draw upon the social services (for example welfare clinics and social psychologists). For their part, the childrome staff would have the opportunity to guide parents in matters of upbringing. The quantity of learning considered to be in the child's best interests would be decided jointly by child, parents, childrome and school – perhaps with the proviso that the child attend agreed school subjects for at least a complete school term. Of course exceptions to this rule would be possible. During school hours, the child would be expected to return to the childrome after completing his/her lessons. No lessons would be given in the childrome itself, with the possible exception of individual tuition on a voluntary basis for those unable to profit at all from school. Supervision and facilities would be available at specified times for completing homework should this be unavoidable. Responsibility for child participation in external social projects and the local municipality would be transferred to the childrome.

For the reasons already indicated, education towards emotional and social maturity cannot flourish within the walls of a school building, not to mention the unhealthy emotional climate prevalent in schools. Allied to freedom from lessons, childromes would give children the opportunity to live their lives in a way appropriate to their stage of development, for which purpose open areas, playing equipment, trees to climb, water, earth, fire, materials to build huts etc. are required. The childrome would also provide homely rooms for playing, craft work, painting, reading, dancing and for meetings, as well as rooms for the staff, and remain open after school hours, at weekends and in the school holidays.

Although some form of training in democracy is probably necessary in a democratic society, such training is almost completely lacking in our school system.

Whilst the so-called "citizenship classes" may be a valuable addition to the curriculum, learning *about* democracy is not the same as actually *practicing* it. Likewise, the debating societies upheld by the old public schools and by some grammar schools, while valuable in training debating and oratory skills, cannot compare with the actual practice of democracy in a living community.

In the course of the child's daily life, real

problems constantly arise that call for a just solution and require resolution. These needs can best be met by instituting a children's parliament in which children can gain direct experience of democracy. A suitable prototype is the children's parliament in Summerhill (which, incidentally, has also been employed therapeutically to treat severe maladjustment (4)). As at Summerhill, the children's parliament would have jurisdiction over matters directly affecting the children. In it, staff and children would each have one vote. Of course the staff would have many other duties such as administration of the childrome and consultation with other institutions, for which the children's parliament would not be responsible. For reasons of brevity, no further organisational details will be listed here, the reader being referred for these to the relevant literature. Note that the childrome is not conceived entirely on uncharted territory, for its constituent parts have already been tried and tested in a range of different constellations over several decades.

CHAPTER 11:
COUNTRIES WHERE CHILDROMES MAY BE NEEDED

The childrome, which was conceived mainly with Great Britain and Germany in mind, would possibly not be appropriate here in Switzerland (or not in all regions), since many old-style village schools, with children of all ages in a single class, still exist. However, the childrome could very well be of special interest to Japanese parents and teachers, because in Japan the education system is highly authoritarian, and the introduction of childromes in Japan would avoid the need for oppositional Japanese parents to send their children almost half way around the world to Summerhill in England to escape this situation, and the cultural displacement that this inevitably involves. In fact, there exist long-standing ties between Summerhill and Japan, going back to Neill's time. On one occasion I can remember, Neill's Japanese translator and supporter, Seishi Shimoda, visited Summerhill.

Britain, Germany and Japan are the main countries that stand to benefit from the introduction of childromes. Childromes could also be considered elsewhere following a careful evaluation of the educational situation applying in the country concerned.

CHAPTER 12: INTRODUCTION OF CHILDROMES INTO THE EXISTING SCHOOL SYSTEM

To introduce childromes into the national education system, the government or the local authority could invite applications from parents and teachers to set up childromes in conjunction with their local schools.

Of course, the final form of the childrome could not be achieved in one step. It would take many years before the public would be willing to accept such an unusual, if perfectly reasonable, solution. However the introduction of childromes could be carried out in stages, the initial stages being relatively simple to realise:

Stage (1) Foundation of a large number of childromes for use outside of school hours. This would provide a platform for political action to achieve the necessary legislative changes; persuasion of parents from all social walks to take part, and establishment of school contacts come within this stage. If requested, parents could receive assistance in dealing with school authorities and individual teachers. The first attempts of many children to associate constructively with one-another would also take place at this stage.

Stage (2) In agreement with schools, release of certain children from school during sport and gymnastics. This stage is necessary in order to demonstrate that not being at school can function in practice.

Stage (3) In this third stage – even without legislative changes – certain subjects could be omitted for some children in favour of the childrome, provided a welfare clinic or private psychologist could show the child were overburdened with schoolwork.

It would be most effective for stages 1 to 3 to be carried out by parents' action groups and not within the framework of official demonstration projects, since, as previous experience has shown, official projects are always liable to be misused for political purposes and/or stopped by withdrawal of funding.

Stage (4) Here, children would be required to attend only those subjects agreed in advance between child, parents, childrome and school. During the longer free periods, children would return to the childrome, for which purpose childromes might need their own minibus. For this stage, the change in the law making education but not school compulsory is essential.

POSTSCRIPT

Children who went to school of their own free will would, by way of enhanced motivation, soon improve the atmosphere of school life: they would no longer need the pressure of examinations to do school work. In case the child's motivation proved insufficient, he/she could be asked to leave the course. This would be an incalculable advantage to the teacher, since little-interested and disruptive children would remain away from class. As in this case it could safely be assumed that all course participants had reached an acceptable standard, the examination could be substituted by a certificate of participation (which is common practice in adult education). Those who doubt this are counselled to place more faith in the child's natural desire to learn and accomplish.

The school would then have to become accustomed to measuring success not in terms of the level of examination results, but in terms of the enthusiasm of pupils for class work. It is my belief that at some future time, when schools are bustling with self-motivated children, many teachers will decide to adopt cooperative teaching methods. Firstly, because they themselves regard them as better, and secondly, because the children demand them. Unsuitable teachers would attract few or no pupils to their classes, motivating them to leave the teaching profession. Under the new system, children would presumably take fewer subjects than is usual at present, leading to a surplus of teachers and overcapacity of school buildings. To forestall this, a sufficient number of places in teacher training colleges would have to be converted to the training of childrome staff, and some schools would have to be divided into a school part and a childrome part (both of course under separate administration). As a consolation, the school, like the universities, could evolve into a pure teaching institution with no explicit social mandate.

The efforts by former Conservative Education Secretary Michael Gove and other politicians to reform the English school system suffer from a tragic misconception of education that confuses a part of education (the learning part) with the whole - a distressing and inexcusable mistake!

The government reformers would be well advised to take every care to ensure that their ill-conceived efforts to raise school learning standards are not unwittingly blighting or wrecking the childhoods of countless children of the nation!

Where the new free schools are concerned, it is early days to judge what might be their future status. It would therefore be premature to speculate on how they might interact with the childromes. Despite this uncertainty, I would suggest the new free schools should embrace the childromes as equal partners in the provision of a *full education programme*, offer the childromes every conceivable support, and keep all options with regard to future cooperation with them open.

All other schools, whether "free" or not, are encouraged to follow this example and to cooperate in the same way with the childromes.

ABOUT THE AUTHOR

Peter Case was born in 1940 at Hertford, England, and spent 10 years at Summerhill as a pupil (1946-56). He graduated in 1964 as a mechanical engineer at Hatfield Polytechnic and obtained a doctorate in fluid dynamics at Liverpool University in 1971. From 1968 till

1977 he was employed as a mechanical engineer in German industry, and from 1977 till early 1980 worked as house husband. After that he worked in Germany and Switzerland as a freelance consulting engineer, and is now a self-employed technical translator for German and English. He is the

father of two grown-up children and lives in Switzerland. The author can be contacted by email at:
peter.case@mhs-mail.ch (from Sept. 2012).

LITERATURE

1. **Hemmings, Ray.** *Fifty Years of Freedom.* London : Allen and Unwin, 1972.

2. **Lane, Homer.** *Talks to parents and teachers.* Cited in: Hemmings, Ray, Fifty Years of Freedom, London, Allen and Unwin, 1972.

3. **Cuddihy, Mikey.** *A Conversation About Happiness - The Story of a Lost Childhood.* London : Atlantic Books, 2014.

4. **Case, Howard W.** *Loving Us.* Westhorpe, Stowmarket, England : private publication (In English), 1978.

5. **Neill, A.S.** *Theorie und Praxis der*

antiautoritären Erziehung. Hamburg : Rowohlt, 1969.

6. **Neill, A. S.** *Summerhill: A Radical Approach To Child Rearing.* New York : Hart Publishing Co., Inc., 1960.

7. **Mayer, Frederick.** *A History of Educational Thought.* Columbus, Ohio :

Charles E. Merill Books, Inc., ca.1950.

8. **Palmer, Joy A., ed.** *Fifty Modern Thinkers on Education- From Piaget to the Present.* Abingdon, Oxon. : Routledge, 2001.

9. **Janov, Arthur.** *The Primal Scream.* New York : Dell Publishing Company, 1970.

10. **anon.** *Education Act.* London : HMSO.,

1944 (Note: the latest Education Act is dated 1996).

11. **anon.** *Home schooling.* unspecified : Wikipedia, 2014.

12. **Palmer, Joy A. ed.** *Fifty Major Thinkers on Education from Confucius to Dewey.* Abingdon, Oxon. : Routledge, 2013.

13. **Hentig, Hartmut von.** article in: Der Spiegel vol.30 no.23, p. 49, 31.5.1976.

14. **Glockseeschule.** *Glockseeschule.* Frankfurt : article in: Frankfurter Rundschau 15.2.1979.

15. **Illich, Ivan.** *Deschooling Society.* Univ. California : Harper & Row, 1971.

In German: Entschulung der Gesellschaft, Hamburg, Rowohlt, 1973.

16. **Kolodziej, Viktor.** *Der Hort als schulbegleitende sozialpädagogische Einrichtung.* In: Kindergarten Heute vol. 7 no. 1 pp. 22-27, 1977.

17. **Plaschke, Angelika.** *Der Hort - eine vernachlässigte Institution.* In: Sozialpädagogische Blätter, pp. 45-50,1977.

18. **Rappen, Elisabeth.** *Hort – eine sozialpädagogische Antwort auf die psychosoziale Lage des Schulkindes.* : In: Theorie und Praxis der Sozialpädagogik

Parts I, II and III, 1977.

19. **Stauch, Ursula.** *Der Kinderhort und seine sozialpädagogischen Aufgaben in der Gegenwart.* Donauwörth : Auer, 1977.

20. **Bronfenbrenner, Uri.** *Is early intervention effective? Facts and principles of*

early intervention: a summary in: Ann M. Clark and A.D.B.Clark (eds.) Early Experience: Myth and Evidence. London : Open Books (in English), 1976.

21. **Weber-Kellermann, Ingeborg.** *Die deutsche Familie.* Frankfurt a. M. : Suhrkamp, 1974.

22. **Johansen, Erna M.** *Betrogene Kinder, eine Sozialgeschichte der Kindheit.* Frankfurt a. M. : Fischer, 1978.

23. **Neill, A.S.** *Summerhill For and Against.* New York : Hart Publishing Co., Inc., 1970.

FURTHER READING

Croall, Jonathan. *Neill of Summerhill, The Permanent Rebel.* unknown : Routledge & Kegan Paul, 1983.

Hemmings, Ray. *Children's freedom; A. S. Neill and the evolution of the Summerhill idea.* unknown : Schocken Books, 1973.

Key, Ellen. *The Century of the Child.* unknown : G.P. Putnam's Sons, 1909.

Neill, A. S. *The Problem Parent.* unknown : Herbert Jenkins, 1932.

Neill, A. S. *Hearts Not Heads in the School.* unknown : Herbert Jenkins, 1945.

Neill, A.S. *Summerhill For and Against.* New

York : Hart Publishing Co., Inc., 1970.

Neill, A.S. *Neill! Neill! Orange Peel!* unknown : Weidenfeld & Nicolson, 1973.

Johansen, Erna M. *Betrogene Kinder, eine Sozialgeschichte der Kindheit.* Frankfurt a. M. : Fischer, 1978.